DEDICATION

To our wonderful Care for the Family Partners –
you are changing lives. Thank you!

the

REALLY

really

brilliant

GRANDPARENTS

with love
Ka—

with love!
Rob

the
LITTLE BOOK FOR
REALLY
really
brilliant
GRANDPARENTS

Rob Parsons & Katharine Hill

Muddy
Pearl

First published in 2020 by Muddy Pearl, Edinburgh, Scotland.

www.muddypearl.com
books@muddypearl.com

© Care for the Family

Cartoons © David McNeill 2020

Rob Parsons and Katharine Hill have asserted their right under the Copyright, Designs and Patents Act 1988 to be identified as the authors of this work.

British Library Cataloguing in Publication Data.
A catalogue record for this book is available from the British Library

ISBN 978-1-910012-98-7

Typeset and designed by Revo Creative Ltd. www.revocreative.co.uk

Printed and bound in Latvia by Livonia Print

ACKNOWLEDGEMENTS

Thanks once again go to our whole team at Care for the Family. Our editor at Care for the Family, Sarah Rowlands, has done a brilliant job, and we are so grateful again to David McNeill for his wonderful cartoons. Many thanks finally to Stephanie and Richard Heald and the team at Muddy Pearl – we love working with you!

So you're either a grandparent or about to become one. Congratulations! Somebody once said that grandchildren are God's reward for everything we had to endure at the hands of our kids. That certainly fits in our case. I have two children and Katharine has four, and although they were perfect darlings for the majority of their childhood, that didn't stop them hiding fish fingers under settee covers, vomiting in supermarket aisles and driving us crazy with fear as teenagers when they were out way past the agreed time.

Although we rang their mobiles incessantly, they were unable to answer because 'There's no phone signal in Jack's house.' On further interrogation the next day it turned out that not only was the phone signal not in Jack's house, neither was our child – he was out at a party!

But even if you share similar memories, all that is in the distant past and your child has just announced that they are about to become a parent. Your first thought may well be: 'I'm not ready to be a grandparent! I'm too young/tired/broke.' But somehow you stifle all those feelings and say, 'Wow – a baby!'

Then the moment comes when you hold that little one for the first time, and you know that you would not only immediately give your life for them, but you already like them more than you did your own kids.

You are a grandparent.

Fortunately in these modern times you can choose what kind of grandparent you want to be. Of course, if you want to, you can immediately slip into the stereotype, acquiring slippers with pom-poms on them and rustling up jam tarts. But these days there are plenty of grandmothers running companies and grandfathers in rock bands. You don't have to be your grandad's grandad!

Whatever style you choose, whether you live around the corner from your children or whether your grandparenting will more often take the form of video calls, you have the incredible privilege of investing some of your time and love into this young life.

*Katharine and I have sifted through stuff we've written over the years, talks we've given, conversations we've had, and put that material together with some of our favourite quotes and David McNeill's wonderful illustrations. We are sure that you are or will be a brilliant grandparent anyway. But we hope this little book will bring you a smile, some encouragement when you feel you're struggling, and above all help you earn that ultimate accolade of grandparenting given by one ten-year-old: 'My grandparents are so old I think they should be dead by now! But I'm glad they're not because **they are always there for me**.'*

A grandfather was telling his little grandson about the things he did in his own childhood: swinging from a tyre that hung from a tree, pony riding, skating on the pond, picking blackberries. The boy was wide-eyed, taking this all in, and then gave a sigh: 'I wish I'd got to know you sooner!'

There are all kinds of grandparents. Yes, there are still grandfathers who, after ten minutes with little Amy and Jack, slip back out to the allotment and leave them with Grandma – who interrupts her baking, wipes the flour from her hands onto her pinafore and gathers them to her bosom for a story. But there are also grandmothers who play in rock bands, run multinational corporations, and skydive; and there are grandfathers who are still under the impression that they should be asked for ID when they buy a bottle of wine in the local supermarket.

We remember with stunning clarity the moment
our dearest told us the news: 'Mum, Dad – Laura
and I are having a baby.' Looking back, we seem to
recall mumbling, 'A baby!' (as if it were one of several
possibilities – a giraffe, for example) and 'Wonderful!'
But our brains were trying to handle hundreds of other
thoughts: 'Yipes! Poor kid!' or, 'Never mind having
children – did you finish that geography homework?'
and, 'I'm not sure I'm ready for this.'

It's an important moment when you get the news that you are going to be a grandparent. Your children will remember your reaction forever. Practise in front of the bathroom mirror not just what you will say, but how you will look when that occasion arrives.

Comments such as 'Can you afford it?' or 'I thought you were saving for a Ford Focus?' are not recommended. In fact, just in case you are, at the moment, only a potential grandparent ... let me give you two words that will stand you in great stead when that incredible event occurs. Begin practising them now. They are, simply, 'Wow!' and 'Brilliant!'

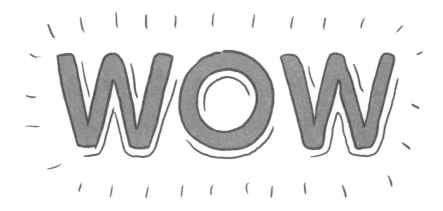

I felt quite nervous about meeting our first grandson, just hours after he was born. I've never been the type to gush over other people's babies, and so I didn't think I'd be a very good grandma. But as soon as they put him in my arms, everything changed. I was a grandmother – and I loved it!

Of course we want to visit as much as possible. We want to help – and 'just have a quick cuddle, while I'm here'. But sometimes the help that is born out of such good intentions can become claustrophobic for the new parents.

With so many people involved, it's as well to remember that it's not a competition – for best gifts, most visits, or who the child most looks like. So when you see the child for the first time, try to resist the temptation to bag this new baby for your side of the family with comments like, 'Oh, look at that chin. He's a Wingsbottom!'

All that's required is, 'What a beautiful baby!' Nor is this the time to mention unusual features. 'What a conk!' may well be true, but is generally not a good way to start.

In medieval times, criminals were put in stocks and pillories. Apparently one poor soul complained that the biggest problem was not that people threw rotten eggs at him, but that his relatives could visit when he had no chance of getting away. It can feel a bit like that for new parents after the birth of a baby. They are at the mercy of anybody who knocks on their door bearing a cuddly toy and a knitted hat.

Children who say to their mother, 'Where did I come from?' are searching for more than biological answers. As we grow, we want to know what our place is in the world. 'How did I get here? How do I fit?' And although in life we are so often consumed with the demands of the present or worries for the future, for answers to some of the very deepest questions we have to go back. We have to discover our roots.

Nobody can help us more in that task than our grandparents. They are holders of the memories, the stories, the ups and downs of life that have been woven together over generations to make up our family. Those memories can provide part of the structure on which young children can build their life. They help to give a sense of 'belonging' and, therefore, security.

When my granddaughter was five, I took her to pick up a relative who was coming to her birthday party. Aunty Margaret was generally cross-tempered, disapproving and went about life with her lips pursed. My granddaughter talked excitedly about what my husband and I had given her for her birthday. Aunty Margaret soon interrupted her. 'You're spoilt!' she hissed.

'Yes, I know,' my granddaughter replied after a short pause. 'Grandma and Grandpa do spoil me – **and I like it!***'*

Share the past with your grandchildren. Take them to see your old home, tell them about anything at all that was significant to you: your first school, your first job, the first time you kissed their grandfather. Don't let the cynicism of the world rob you or your grandchildren of these moments. Have the courage to grasp hold of them for yourself – and to pass them on.

HAVE FUN – MAKE
YOUR GRANDCHILDREN
LAUGH. REMEMBER
THAT 'BORING' IS FAR
WORSE THAN 'BATTY'.

THE LITTLE BOOK FOR REALLY ...

Even young grandparents seem enormously old to a small child, although the child may politely deny it. One small girl, feeling proud of reaching the monumental age of four, turned to her young-looking grandmother and asked, 'How come I'm so old if you're so new?'

ALISON JUDSON RYERSON

I always cleaned the children's shoes –
the little (tiny!) patent shoes,
that covered feet fresh out of booties –
cleaned the black and made it shine,
removing traces of stewed prune
and other culinary delights known only to the very young.

And as they grew, I cleaned a larger shoe.
Shoes that were strong enough to walk in, almost!
Certainly strong enough for a toddler to take five
steps ... and fall.

And then those first school shoes,
shoes which led little feet
into a world full of such tomorrows.

But children grow.
And shoes are for feet that move,
that take the boy into a man.
And I remember well the evening that I came
with cloth and brush, as I had done so many times,
only to discover that, of course, the shoes had gone.

Oh, not for cleaning now –
other hands have long since done that task.
No, they will bring a man to me and a woman
holding the hands of tiny ones
with little feet.
And young eyes will look up and say,
'Grandpa, Mummy said ... that you will clean my shoes.'

Psychologists describe the relationship
between a grandparent and grandchild
as 'an emotionally uncomplicated form
of love'. Parents might complain that it's
easier for grandparents. They don't have
the twenty-four-hour-a-day hassles, the
cross patches and, sometimes in the
teenage years, the unremitting rudeness
that so often comes attached to puberty.
Because they don't have to deal with the
normal responsibilities of parenthood their
task is, in many ways, much easier and the
relationship quite different.

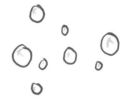

ONE CHILD PUT IT LIKE THIS: 'BEING WITH MY NAN IS LIKE HAVING A BATH THAT IS FULL OF BUBBLES FILLED WITH LOVE AND WITH NO COLD BITS.'

Perhaps the greatest repository of the past is the photo album. Explain to your grandchildren who the people are and tell their stories. Show them pictures of their parents – toothless and grinning on assorted beaches – and of fearsome aunties and crazy uncles.

One grandmother told us that her granddaughter never tires of looking at her wedding album. Every time the child opens it she says the same thing, 'You look beautiful, Nanny, but Grampy looks funny.'

TRY TO CARVE OUT SOME
PRECIOUS TIME FOR EACH
GRANDCHILD, ONE TO ONE. IT
MAY NOT ALWAYS BE POSSIBLE,
BUT SPENDING TIME WITH
THEM INDIVIDUALLY ALLOWS AN
OPPORTUNITY TO GET CLOSE.

The role of a grandparent in an adolescent's life can be remarkable. Grandparents don't have to come up with solutions: so often their power is in simply listening. Don't underestimate the power of a grandparent in the life of a teenager. Some experts have called grandparents 'an emotional safety net' for teenagers – somebody who will not just help them get through the teenage years, but who will shape their lives for ever.

THE LITTLE BOOK FOR REALLY ...

An eight-year-old, commenting on what was great about her grandmother, put it like this:

Grandmothers are people who don't have children of their own. They don't have to do anything except be there.

If they take us for walks, they slow down past things like pretty leaves and caterpillars and they never say, 'Hurry up!'

Grandmothers don't have to be clever – just to be able to answer questions like 'Why isn't God married?'

Everyone should have a grandmother – they are the only grown-ups that have time.

IF OUR CHILDREN ARE GOING THROUGH DIVORCE OR SEPARATION, A GRANDPARENT CAN BE A PORT IN THE STORM FOR THEIR GRANDCHILDREN.

If we are wise as grandparents we will hold our advice – brilliant though we're sure it is – until that defining moment when it will be welcomed. In other words, when we're asked for it. Having said that, really wily grandparents will sometimes manage to slip in a little advice without their kids even realizing. One grandmother has a brilliant line: 'Not much good asking me, love, it's all so long ago, it's a bit of a blur ... but I seem to remember this working ...'

'I remember gazing at my own babies for the first time and feeling a little shy, it was almost as if they were strangers. But the second I saw my grandchild – from that very first moment, I was overwhelmed with love.'

Grandma always made you feel like she had been waiting to see just you all day and now the day was complete.

MARCY DEMAREE

Job Description: Grandparent

- Lifetime position with responsibility for grandchildren from birth to beyond maturity.

- To work under supervision of directors of family-oriented organization that may or may not be anticipating expansion. Not a 9-to-5 job. May involve some travel.

- Social media experience not necessary – in five years' time grandchild will provide training.

- Skill in reading aloud essential.

- Successful applicant may have multiple duties and functions as required: caregiver, nurturer, playmate, teacher, spiritual guide, cheerleader.

- Individual must be loving, caring, loving, selfless, loving, accepting and ... loving

Author unknown

Always

'My Grandad always rings me on a Monday night.'

'My Nan sends me a letter every Friday.'

'My Grampy never forgets my birthday.'

'When I go to visit Gran in the summer holidays she makes a big tent out of the sheets on the bed and we tell stories in it and eat chocolate.'

Of course, it's also true that with modern technology the task of grandparenting at a distance is easier than ever. 'Pops and I always sing "Bring Me Sunshine" together when we finish talking on the phone.'

Be honest about your own trials as a parent – let your children know that it's not just them struggling with some element of parenting. It's a little easier to handle a baby that's crying half the night if you know that others have gone through this and come out the other end.

One grandmother made a brightly coloured wrap that had an outline of her own hands at either end. She told her granddaughter that at any time she could ask her mum to curl it around her and she would feel her nan's arms hugging her. She had no idea how important the present would become to a very insistent two-year-old. Every night, just as her grandmother in Scotland is waking up, a small child in Sydney, Australia falls off to sleep with her nan's 'arms' wrapped tightly around her.

My grandmother really loves me. Even though I live hundreds of miles away from her, I talk to her almost every day. Sometimes she sends me stickers for my collection and she sends me jokes on my phone. Every year I spend a week with her and we have such a laugh. I think when I'm older I would like to live near my gran.

EMILY, AGED 8

Across the miles

You can still have a strong relationship with your grandchildren. You can foster love and deep relationships. You can pass on values and encouragement. There is no doubt that it's harder to grandparent at a distance – and perhaps, therefore, we have to try harder than those for whom it's not an issue. But the great encouragement, of which we should never lose sight, is this:

LOVE TRAVELS WELL.

My granddaughter came to spend a few weeks with me, and I decided to teach her to knit. She watched me solemnly, mouth open, as I cast on and knitted the first few rows in stocking stitch. I was rather pleased at the impression I was making, and decided to show off a bit by creating a fancy pattern. My granddaughter seemed to be enthralled, watching carefully and examining the knitting as it grew.

Suddenly she stood up, put her hands on her hips and shook her head disbelievingly: 'Nanna, you mean you can do all that, but you can't work my Playstation?'

After putting her small grandchildren to bed, Gran slipped into old trousers and a huge, droopy, stained T-shirt and proceeded to wash her hair. The children started talking and playing in the dark and after several shouted attempts to quieten them, she finally lost patience. She wrapped a towel around her head and stormed into their room, putting them back to bed with stern warnings.

As she left the room, she heard the three-year-old say with a trembling voice, 'Who was that?'

WHATEVER AGE OUR GRANDCHILDREN ARE, THIS IS NOT ABOUT BEING ABLE TO ENTERTAIN THEM SO WELL THEY WOULD READILY CHOOSE A CHAT WITH US OVER PLAYING ON THEIR XBOX. IT'S ABOUT GIVING THEM THE DIGNITY OF BELIEVING THAT THEY MATTER.

An elderly grandmother went to watch her grandson at the school sports day. Tom didn't get into the final of the 100 metres or the 200 metres, and he was unplaced in the longer races as well. In fact, the only event in which he looked remotely comfortable was the egg-and-spoon race, but even then he came last.

As Tom and his grandmother walked away together, the little boy's head was down until she put her arm around him and whispered,

'You were the only one whose egg didn't fall off the spoon.'

Imagine having somebody who could make you feel so special. Somebody who would 'eat' with relish the plastic sausages you cooked for dinner, who gave you a hug when you didn't make the team, who listened for weeks on end to the story of your first romance, and made you hot chocolate when it ended. Imagine somebody with time to pass on traditions and values ... to write to you, to ring you – even, perhaps, to pray for you.

When grandparenting works best, it does so as a support to both parents and children. Free of the daily routines, discipline issues and major responsibilities, grandparents can more easily make a child feel special.

One small child said, 'Grandmas don't just say, "That's nice". They roll their eyes and throw up their hands and smile big! You get your money's worth out of grandmas.'

Birthing pools, sleep apps, video monitors, sensor mats, white noise, baby led weaning ... there will be different ways of doing things than when we were parents. Where possible, embrace them – the old ways aren't always the best.

OUR KIDS CAN PROBABLY SURVIVE
WITHOUT OUR ADVICE, BUT
THEY DESPERATELY NEED OUR
AFFIRMATION. FIND THINGS YOU
CAN PRAISE IN YOUR CHILD'S
PARENTING.

But if it's true that life in modern families can sometimes be more complicated than in previous generations, it's also true that most grandparents desperately want to be involved in their grandchildren's lives. In a world where so many people – especially young people – feel insecure and somewhat disconnected, children need their grandparents.

In societies where family life is strong, the elderly are listened to; they're allowed to tell the stories of their life to the young, and they are honoured. There's a recognition that grandparents play an important part in the task of helping children take their place in society.

Aim for consistency when you're looking
after your grandkids. Try to agree a joint
policy with their parents on rules for
screens, sweets, bedtimes, discipline and
so on (though you could probably allow for
the odd sneaky chocolate biscuit!).

IT'S NOT IMPOSSIBLE
TO HAVE A GOOD
RELATIONSHIP WITH
YOUR GRANDCHILD,
EVEN IF YOU FIND IT
CHALLENGING TO GET
ALONG WITH YOUR
CHILD'S PARTNER.

The grandchildren were always delighted to see her. Why? They enjoyed her because she obviously enjoyed them.

**PEREGRINE CHURCHILL,
GRANDSON OF LADY RANDOLPH
CHURCHILL**

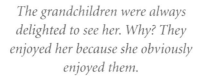

Grandmothers don't talk baby talk to us like visitors do, because they know it's hard for us to understand it. When they read to us, they don't skip pages, or mind if it's the same story over and over again. Everybody should try to have a grandma, especially if you don't have Netflix.

The gifts of love and acceptance help the grandchild achieve something absolutely vital for strong growth into adulthood: emotional health. In a world where friends can be cruel and teachers sometimes have to say negative things, it's good to have somebody who believes in you anyway.

Whether it is an eight-year-old who has been left out of the team or a fifteen-year-old who has been the butt of a joke on a WhatsApp group, grandparents can give children reassurance, encouragement and wise advice over the years. They have it in their power to give their grandchildren an incredible gift: the reassurance that they are loved simply for who they are.

One granny we know has written a lovely story with her grandchild. One of them would write a paragraph, then email it over to the other, who would write the next paragraph, and so on. It was not only a fun activity, but it built what is now a very special relationship between them.

Whether grandparents engage with their grandchildren face-to-face or across the miles, use of digital devices will almost certainly play a part. One grandmother was delighted to receive this message from her granddaughter: 'Dear Granny, thanks for my present. Love from me and my new app.'

WISE GRANDPARENTS KNOW THAT IN TRUTH THEIR ROLE HAS CHANGED: THEY HAVE MOVED FROM BEING THE COACH AT THE SIDE OF THE TRACK TO SHOUTING ENCOURAGEMENT FROM THE GRANDSTAND.

Even – and perhaps especially – in this technological age, children love to receive letters. A real piece of paper, with real writing and your very own name on the envelope is enough to make any eight-year-old feel special.

Our grandchildren accept us for ourselves, without rebuke or effort to change us, as hardly anyone else has ever done.

THE REASON GRANDPARENTS AND GRANDKIDS GET ALONG SO WELL IS BECAUSE THEY HAVE A COMMON ADVERSARY.

Research shows that a close relationship between grandparents and grandchildren can act as a 'buffer' against the adverse effects of some life events, such as parental separation. It's not surprising. In a world where everything seems to have shifted, grandparents can give a sense of stability. At these times the simple repetition of the traditions that always go on at 'Grandma's house' – stories, treats, games, reading and fun – can help steady a young life that is rocking at that moment.

Of course, sometimes we are separated by long distances from our grandchildren, so here are a couple of ideas to help build a good relationship across the miles:

Record stories for your grandchildren that their parents can play to them. It could be an event from your life or a story from one of their favourite books.

Send pictures of yourself to your grandchildren, and/or video call them regularly, to remind them what you look like.

Take photos on your smartphone of your home, work, hobbies, pets, and send them to your grandchildren, perhaps on a family WhatsApp chat. It will help your grandchildren to feel they 'know' you.

Send notes or postcards to your grandchildren now and again, and encourage them to write back – finger paintings or foot/handprints that you can put on the fridge are particularly lovely.

The values we pass on to our grandchildren
are not only taught – but caught.

When you thought I wasn't looking,
I saw you hang my first painting on the refrigerator,
and I immediately wanted to paint another one.

When you thought I wasn't looking,
I saw you make my favourite cake for me,
and I learned that the little things can be the special
things in life.

When you thought I wasn't looking,

I saw that you cared,

and I wanted to be everything that I could be.

When you thought I wasn't looking,

I looked at you and wanted to say,

'Thanks for all the things I saw when you thought I

wasn't looking.'

Grandkids bring you into a sweeter, slower present. They show you the future at a time when a lot of your friends are thinking about the past. And they take you back to childhood – theirs, the parent's, your own: a three-time admittance to wonderland.

My grandchild has taught me what true love means. It means watching Peppa Pig *while Arsenal vs Liverpool is on the other channel.*

There is a saying: 'When an old person dies, it is as if a library burns down.' But the library shouldn't burn down. One of the most valuable things a grandparent can do is to record the past for future generations – so make sure you record it. Remember, when you do this, it's not your problem to edit out the boring bits; that task is for others, later. Your job is simple: to take out a little fire insurance on that library.

'You look lovely today.'

'I think you could end up playing for
Manchester United.'

'You're a wonderful cook' (to that four-year-
old and her plastic three-course dinner).

Are these statements all true? No. Do the
children believe the judgement? When they
are young – yes. When they are older – maybe
not. But that later realisation will not rob the
words of their power, for by then, they will
have done their job.

GRANDMA TAUGHT ME
HOW TO CROCHET AND
TO KNIT, HOW TO PRAY
AND EVEN HOW TO MAKE
CHOCOLATE CAKE!

Over the years, we've had the opportunity of talking with thousands of individuals about their childhood, and time and again those who spoke of strong families also spoke of traditions. Whether these families were rich or poor, lived in the country or the city, their response was often the same. When we asked them to tell us what made the memories of their family life sweet, sooner or later they'd start a sentence with, 'We always ...'

Make traditions with your grandchildren. Those who are young remember the things we do over and over again with them, even though the actual time spent on them is small.

I stopped outside our grandson's door at bedtime and heard his mummy saying the same little prayer I used to say with her every night when she was a child.

'Lord keep us safe this night,

secure from all our fears.

May angels guard us as we sleep

'til morning light appears.'

Grandparents are the holders of the
memories, the stories that have been
woven together over generations to make
up our family.

Something magical happens when parents turn into grandparents. Their attitude changes from 'money doesn't grow on trees' to spending it like it does.

PAUL LINDEN

New technology can really help families connect over distances or during times when meeting in person might not be possible. You don't have to be a tech whiz – your grandchildren can teach you that – but mastering the basics of Zoom, FaceTime or other video chat platforms can really help grow your relationship with your grandchild. If they get restless half way through the call and start jumping on the sofa or doing headstands, don't worry, it doesn't have to last for ages – it's the connection that counts.

Be spontaneous once in a while – have
a teddy bears' picnic on the living room
floor, a water fight in the garden or turn the
garden into a sports arena.

Whether it's helping our children realize that their feelings of exhaustion or inadequacy are normal, and giving reassurance that they are doing the best they can, spotting the signs of post-natal depression or an issue with the baby, grandparents can be a powerful resource for new parents to draw on. Being available – whether by phone, text or in person – is hugely important.

IF I HAD KNOWN GRANDCHILDREN WERE SO MUCH FUN, I'D HAVE HAD THEM FIRST!

IT CAN BE HARD NOT BEING ABLE TO SEE YOUR GRANDCHILDREN. BE CREATIVE AND TAKE EVERY OPPORTUNITY YOU CAN TO CONNECT WITH THEM AND LET THEM KNOW YOU ARE INTERESTED IN THEIR LIVES.

Being a new parent is tough and our children will go through all kinds of emotions. Let's try not to get caught up in the drama, stay calm, and bring perspective and encouragement.

One grandfather asked his eight-year-old granddaughter what she wanted to be when she grew up. She replied, 'Retired, like you, Grandpa!'

WHAT IS LOVE?

Genuine love is not just about feelings but
actually doing things – love in action. In
our grandparenting, what will count most
is doing things with our grandchildren
and letting them know that we enjoy their
company.

DEALING WITH YOUR OWN WORRIES

When a grandchild is ill, or their parents are going through a hard time, grandparents will experience worry too. Find trusted friends to talk to, and try to keep calm for your children and grandchildren, letting them know that you are there to be called on to help.

Of course, there are challenges in being a grandparent: when to speak, when to be quiet, when to spoil and when to say no. But the rewards are brilliant. You get to be loved by somebody who doesn't care a fig how you look (as long as you aren't totally scary!), what you've achieved or how big your bank balance is – just as long as you can ...

... BUY ICE CREAM!

THE LITTLE BOOK FOR REALLY ...

Care for the Family is a national charity which aims to strengthen family life and help those who face family difficulties. Working throughout the UK and the Isle of Man, we provide marriage and relationship, parenting, and bereavement support through events, courses, a volunteer network, online and other resources. For more information, and to explore our wide range of resources on all aspects of family life, visit our website at **www.cff.org.uk**.